Benchwarmer

What to Do
When You're on the Bench of Life

Ammishaddai Grand-Jean, MPA

Printed in the United States of America

ISBN 978-1-7362630-3-7 (Print-Paperback)
ISBN 978-1-7362630-0-6 (Ebook)

AGJ Speaks, LLC
300 Colonial Center Parkway, STE 100N,
Roswell, GA, 30076, USA
www.agjspeaks.com

To God, family, friends, acquaintances, and the billions of Benchwarmers who are waiting for their turn to shine in the sun. Your time is nearer than you think. Please don't give up.

Contents

Introduction

Typically, people don't read the introduction of a book; at least I don't. So congratulations to you for even taking a glimpse. *Benchwarmer* is a book given to me by God mostly because it relates to my life so well. We all find ourselves on a bench in life. It is different for each person, but it is a bench when you feel that you're stuck or not able to go forward. When you're watching others living your dream. When you want to enter that next phase of life or that promotion, but you feel that everyone is passing you by. Maybe you're single and you've been single for a while and all of your friends around you are dating or married. Maybe you've been working hard at your job and even doing the extra things—you know, like office parties, wishing people happy birthday, coming in early and staying late, but still you haven't been selected for a promotion or a raise. You envision

1

yourself on that stage singing, rapping, or speaking to thousands of people with all the different colors of LED lights on you, but you can barely get 100 views on social media. What do you do when you're on the bench of life? When you're wanting to advance and improve, but you feel that you're barely making progress where you are in life. You've tried all of the self-help books and you've prayed without ceasing, but still no progress. It appears as if Heaven is silent. It appears as if you're just invisible. Everyone else seems to make it so easy, and anything they go after they get after the first try.

These are the same questions and frustrations that I had and brought to God. "Hello?! Heaven? Yes, I'm trying to track my prayer request and know the status of my blessing. Yes, I'll hold." I knew that I was gifted in the areas of speaking and leadership, but I could barely get people to watch my daily motivations and sermons that I would post on social media. I wanted to give up and just settle with being average or just accept that I would always be on the bench. I had family, friends, and even random strangers complimenting and encouraging me, but I blew past them and didn't truly internalize their words. You know the difference of how you feel when your mom says you look handsome/beautiful versus your crush saying it. Oftentimes we focus more on our flaws, mistakes, and imperfections rather than our praiseworthy feats and attributes. In my eyes, I knew where I saw myself. I knew where I wanted to be, but despite all the efforts I made to go forward, I felt stuck. Then, almost as if God dropped the idea from Heaven specifically to my brain, the idea of this book came to mind.

The purpose of this book is to give you another perspective regarding your unique situation. You see, there are things you can do while you're on the bench of life. You and I can't control when or how we'll get off the bench, but there are key lessons to learn while we're there. There are skills you can pick up while being on the bench that will improve your performance when you finally arrive at your dreams. This book is focused on helping you see the blessing that comes with being on the bench. It's not something you hear often. "I'm happy to be on the sidelines," said no one ever. Yet, sometimes, the bench is the best place to be before we enter the arena and stage we've been created for. No, this may not be the news you want to hear, but you've already bought, borrowed, or bootlegged the book so you might as well finish it. God showed me that there are blessings on the bench that we often miss because we stress and spend too much time and energy trying to get off the bench rather than learning while we're there. I want to be obedient to God and share with you the lessons He shared with me. Again, this book is not intended to help you get off of the bench, but to prepare you for the moment *when* you finally get off of it and into the game.

Whether you choose to read the whole book in a day or one chapter at a time, I hope you will enjoy reading this short 'n' sweet treat. Grab a highlighter; you'll need it. Oh, and just a heads-up—some stories may have fake names and be exaggerated for confidentiality, humor, and to drive a point home. Okay, enough introduction. Let's start.

Fix Your Attitude

*"You must have the same attitude that Christ
Jesus had."*
—Philippians 2:5 NLT

*"The greatest discovery of all time is that
a person can change his future by merely
changing his attitude."*
—Oprah Winfrey

"Pardon the interruption. I would like to see
these fifteen guys in the gym . . ." My heart
was pounding and my stomach was filled
with butterflies. It was the fall season of my 8th-grade
year. I had tried out for the basketball team despite
the laughs and giggles of my friends. Growing up, I
loved and admired the sport of basketball. I wasn't
ever really that great, but I just loved being active

and participating in any sport. Watching the notorious *High School Musical* only fueled my desire to be on a basketball team and play in a gym filled with people yelling, screaming, crying, and roasting. I could already see my Haitian family taking up a whole section and having T-shirts with my face on it. Of course, there was a special status you got from being on the basketball team. You definitely had a better shot asking a cheerleader out or getting a date to the school dance. I definitely had my challenges getting a girl's attention in those days. A girl leaving me on read was better than the common response, "Boi, bye!"

Thirteen names had already been called out loud and I could see the snickers and the laughs of the guys around me who were getting ready to shower me with "I told you so!" I was already fighting back the tears and rehearsing my excuses so the jokes wouldn't hit too close to home. Then it happened. "And Ammishaddai Grand-Jean. These guys are the new members of our eighth-grade basketball team." I still remember seeing the jaws that dropped and the jealous looks. All I could think of was the list of girls that would start blowing up my mother's phone—I didn't get my own phone until 10th grade.

This was historic. Our school was a public charter school founded in 2009 and we finally were able to assemble our first ever basketball team. From the first practice, I was hustling all over the place. Coming on time, leading the laps around the gym, and encouraging my teammates. Before long, it was time for our first game against the notorious North Clayton Eagles. My dad had happened to teach there a couple years back, and he told me how the students there breathe, eat, and sleep basketball. I was so excited and ready to play and show off my skills in front of my family and especially the cheerleaders. "Grand-Jean! [pronounced *Gron John* by Coach] You'll be playing point guard for third string." I was excited about that even though I saw myself more as a shooting guard, but I was confused about what the coach meant by "third string." After the introductions and warm-ups, the game finally was about to begin and I found myself on the bench. I was shocked at first and thought the coach had made a mistake. So I went on the court and started to guard a player with my arms around him until we almost got a technical foul because we had 6 players on the court. "Grand-Jean, SIT DOWN!" I was embarrassed for a little bit but still began to stretch. I thought the coach just wanted me to rest up and be that explosive 6th man like James Harden back in the day. Five minutes of the game went by and we were down by 20. I got up and asked the coach if I should go in to play. "No, Grand-Jean." Halftime arrived, and the score was 47 to 5. (The 5 points came from free throws.) We were getting annihilated. To be fair, it was our first game in the school's history compared to a school that had competed in state and division tournaments. The coach gave an impassioned speech in the locker room and told the team what we were lacking. "WHAT IS WRONG WITH Y'ALL?! Did you forget what we learned in practice? Did your girl-friend break up with you last night?? If y'all don't git—" The buzzer sounded and saved us from further scolding. I was motivated and excited to finally get in the game, but once again I was told to sit on the bench. Slowly, my optimism receded. As the points of the other team began to rise, so did my disappoint-ment in my coach, my team, and, mostly, myself. All of my hard work, persistence, and the dreams I had were for nothing. The final score was 63 to 13. We lost by 50 points. I was frustrated and disheartened. I felt that even my time during practice was a waste and that I was simply inadequate. It was a long and quiet bus ride back to our school. I sat in the back with my head against the fogged window and wondered when I could finally prove myself. When would coach finally see my talents and abilities? When would I finally get off the bench?

What do you do when you're on the bench? You've practiced your pickup lines, but still can't get a date. You've polished your resume and rehearsed your elevator pitch, but despite getting final-round interviews, you're not selected for that position or promotion. You have decent test scores and glowing recommendations, but you've been rejected from all your top schools. You've made and released several songs, but still can't get your song on the radio or a Spotify playlist. You've taken the bar exam twice already and you don't have the courage to take it again.

Everyone in the world at some point has spent a significant time on the bench. Michael Jackson, Tony

Hawk, Beyoncé, President Barack Obama, Leonardo DiCaprio, Taylor Swift, LeBron James, and so many others have all been on the bench at some point of their lives. Often, we compare the end of someone's book to the beginning of ours. We want to accelerate to the part where we get that Oscar, Nobel Prize, MVP Award, wedding, CEO status, but we fail to realize that life doesn't happen exponentially. Even from nature, we can observe that everything has its own season.

What does it mean to be on the bench of life? Being on the bench means waiting to fulfill that dream, purpose, and goal you envision. You're waiting for an opportunity or a breakthrough to be in that sweet spot where you feel and sense that you are doing what you love and what comes naturally. The bench looks different for everyone because we all have different careers, dreams, ambitions, and purpose, but the sentiments are similar. When you're on the bench, you feel frustrated, useless, stressed, and at times depressed. The bench is a place that everyone enters, but not everyone leaves.

The amount of time that each of us spends on the bench is not and will not be the same, but none of us knows how long we will be there. Oftentimes, people give up right before they are called off of the bench into the game. The actions that we take while we're on the bench determine our performance when we get in the game. That line was good, so go ahead and highlight that. What millions if not billions of people do is spend so much time complaining about being on the bench and trying to find cheap ways to get off that they miss the blessing of being on the bench. Yes, I said blessing. The bench provides the perfect seat and vantage point of the game. You can see and hear the plays made by the players and even see the fouls that occur that the referee doesn't always catch. By missing the blessing of being on the bench, you affect your performance once you actually get in the game.

We pray, fast, and cry out to God asking Him to give us that promotion, to enlarge our territory, to help us attain what we are seeking, and we even remind Him of His scriptures. Yet, God reminded me that "my thoughts are not your thoughts, neither are your ways my ways. . . . As the heavens are higher than the earth, so are my ways higher than your ways and my thoughts higher than your thoughts" (Isaiah 55:8–9

NIV). As I reflect on the time that I spent on the bench during games, I realized that God is the Coach. While He is not flawed or ruthless, as some coaches can be, He truly has a vision, strategy, and a game plan to win. He decides who gets in the game and when they get in. There is a specific plan and purpose that He has for each player. Instead of us seeking to do our will and enact our ideas when we get in the game, we should seek instead to fulfill His plan, purpose, and will. Yet, most times, we come in calling the shots and plays and forget that we are on an invisible clock. You're on the bench of life right now, but there are lessons to learn and different actions that God wants you to take that will favorably impact your performance when you enter the game.

There's so much to break down and discuss, but before we go further, there is one important lesson and practice that everyone should do if they feel that they are on the bench. It sets the tone and is the foundation for all the other actions that will ensue. The first lesson is: **Fix Your Attitude**.

Your attitude is one of the most influential tools you possess that determines your future and success.

While it can seem insignificant, your attitude enables you to do the right things, and even the wrong things. Your attitude affects how you see the world, but most importantly yourself and your value. While being on the bench of life is not the most exciting place to be, your attitude will determine whether you get in the game and how long you'll last once you're in. Let's break it down.

If you're currently on the bench and you're waiting for that moment, promotion, freedom, or your heart's desire, you have to set your attitude in a position that enables you to grow. Many of us think that the true and real change occurs when we're in the game, have that title, or are going on a world tour. In order for true growth to occur, your attitude has to be positive. To waste your time on the bench being mad that you're not in the game can lead to you missing the lessons and blessings of being on the bench. Bringing back Oprah Winfrey's quote, your attitude steers the destiny of your ship. Many times, we succumb to the negative thoughts, such as, "I'll never be good enough; I'll never get married; I'll never start my own company or write that book. I'm not good enough. Why is it easier for everyone else except me?" These thoughts unfortunately take root in us and affect our attitude. We have a distasteful attitude about our current situation and we decide to abort the mission. We decide to leave the bench. Today, our generation is filled with quitters and microwave believers. We want change to happen now. We want to be at that level of success and perfection we envision instantly. Technology has played a large role in shaping our expectations. We constantly compare ourselves to the next person and to people we see on social media. We forget that quality takes time. We forget that there's a difference in quality between fast food and Thanksgiving dinner.

Instead, you have to develop an attitude that is not dependent on your current circumstance, but instead is anchored in where you're going. *That was a really good line—you may want to write that down.* If your attitude is consistent with the end goal you have in mind, then the numerous circumstances won't deter you from achieving your goal. Your attitude is synonymous to the type of gas you put in your car. All gas is not the same. Some can get you to your destination;

however, it ruins the engine of the car or makes it difficult to drive. You need the best attitude possible in order to arrive at the destination you're seeking.

We need to develop an attitude that has patience. It's easy to allow our emotions to fluctuate depending on our situation, and if we do that, we will never be able to grow or get to see what's around the corner. Patience is something that is difficult to practice, but can often save your life. One day my friend and I were on our way to meet up with other friends for dinner. We were at a red light waiting and talking about random things. The light finally turned green. I immediately told my friend to go, but for some reason, she didn't start driving right away. Two seconds later, a red sports car ran the red light. The rest of the car ride was quiet. I reflected on how, if she had listened to me, we would have been T-boned and that would have been the end of my young life. Often, I immediately drive once the light turns green and never think anything of it. It seems insignificant, but having a patient attitude can be a lifesaving decision.

You need to build an attitude of resilience, having enough discipline to endure the storms while you pursue the dreams you've been given. In college, I felt impressed by God to run for student government president at my school. It was a pretty daunting task given that I was a black student at a predominantly white institution with about 27,000 undergraduate students. When I talked to God, I felt that I was supposed to run, but when I asked Him if I would win, there was silence. Regardless, I ran, and despite an amazing campaign, I lost. I was heartbroken and felt defeated. I never wanted to be involved with public service again. The next year, I again felt God telling me to run for president, and this time He showed me that I would be successful. I had this conviction in my heart that I knew God was leading and directing my path. When I announced that I would run for president again, I was met with mixed emotions. Most laughed or were fearful that I would lose again; even I was fearful. My running mates were also black and we were campaigning to be among the highest student leaders on campus. During this pivotal moment in my college career, I had two options: adopt an attitude and mindset of fear or an attitude of determination and persistence.

Having an attitude of fear would have caused me much stress and a poor performance in campaigning and reaching students. Due to fear, I could have decided to drop out and save myself the embarrassment or try to cheat and win the election that way. Instead, I chose to have an attitude of determination and resilience, deciding that I would work hard to be intentional and act as if I were already in the role as I addressed the concerns of each student. In the end, our team won and had the largest voter turnout in the history of the organization.

Your attitude is heavily connected to your "why." Why do you want to be a pilot? Why do you want to be drafted #1? Why do you want to be a Supreme Court Justice? Why is it so important that you buy your mom a house one day or your dad a brand-new car? Our attitudes are often dependent on our why. It's important to take time and reflect on this. Once you are aware of your why, you'll realize that the attitude you have will be essential in order to arrive at your destination. Your why will also shape your attitude into one that can best aid you in making your dreams a reality.

Bad Attitudes Wreck Dreams

Your attitude can even ruin an upcoming blessing with your name on it. I've always wanted a surprise birthday party. I love to plan surprises and see the genuine shock (and sometimes fear) on my friends' faces. I wanted to experience the same bewilderment, but I also did not want to ask someone to plan a surprise birthday for me (it wouldn't be a surprise and that's not very humble). It was a Sunday afternoon and my parents told me that they wanted to take me out to eat for my birthday before I went back to college that night. I assumed that it would be just me and my family so I wanted to get it over with quickly. My brother was in charge of organizing everything, and when we arrived at the first location, there was little to no parking. We waited for my brother to make another suggestion, but because he was taking too long, in my opinion, and I was already hangry and cranky at not having a surprise birthday, I quickly suggested somewhere else that I thought would suffice. Despite my brother's warnings, I pressed on because I thought it was just going to be me and my family. Finally, we arrived at the restaurant and I told the waiter our party size of 6, which included just my family. My mom and dad pleaded with me to wait for my brother, but I didn't listen and was arrogant. Finally, one by one, different friends of mine came through the door and then I realized I had made a serious mistake. The second location that I suggested didn't have space for the 18 people that came to celebrate my birthday. I finally conceded to my brother's recommendation and learned that I had almost ruined my surprise due to my attitude and stubbornness. It was a lesson that I will never forget. How many of us have ruined surprises, blessings, promotions, and new beginnings because of our attitude? What have you allowed your negative attitude to steal or prolong in your life?

I want to make one thing clear: It's OK to be mad. It's OK to get frustrated. Your feelings are valid and natural. We wouldn't have them if they were not important and essential to our lifestyles as humans. However, it's important to remember that feelings are temporary, but attitudes are overarching. You can have an attitude of joy and go through life with a positive mindset, but feel sad or frustrated some days.

Your attitude serves as a compass and directs you as you strive toward your goals, and it is important to maintain a great and sustainable attitude in order to arrive at your destination. Even the world's most renowned chefs have instances of adding too much or forgetting to add a special ingredient. While they may have a moment of frustration due to the pressure of always having to achieve such a high bar of excellence, they maintain a positive attitude.

THE MODEL ATTITUDE

What's the best attitude to have? We need to have an attitude that is patient, optimistic, and humble.

PATIENCE

A patient attitude is needed while you're on the bench. Whining or complaining about how easy things are for others or how you feel that everyone else is passing you by is not going to get you off of the bench. Instead, foster a patient attitude that recognizes that the time you're on the bench is crucial and that soon you will have your turn in the game. A patient attitude is important because it also prevents you from pursuing artificial or shortcut actions in order to get in the game before your time. There's a reason why we all know the saying "Good things come to those who wait"! There's also a reason this quote is cliché—because it's true. A patient attitude recognizes that the valuable time you have while you're on the bench provides you with a chance for self-reflection and solitude, which won't exist as much once you're in the game.

OPTIMISM

An optimistic attitude is important while you're on the bench because you're maintaining a positive mindset that will benefit your performance once you're actually in the game. Don't say things like, "I hope I'm just as good; I hope I don't fumble the ball," while envisioning potential embarrassing moments in your mind. Our mind can be our greatest asset, but also our greatest opposition if we don't control it. Surround yourself with encouraging people and resources to nurture a positive mindset before you enter the "game" of your life. Don't hang around people who have been or are in salty and toxic relationships. While you think it's going to help you to know what not to do, you become discouraged and even pick up the habits and language of those negative people. Instead, have an optimistic attitude that puts faith in who you are and who created you. Often, we're afraid of being optimistic because we don't want to be disappointed. We would rather be pessimistic so we can guard our hearts and emotions. That's a terrible way to live because we attract what we think and what we say. When has having a negative attitude been beneficial to anyone in achieving their dreams or goals?

HUMILITY

Finally, a humble attitude is key to have on the bench. Don't assume that you're better than those who are actually in the game. I would often sit on the bench and tell myself how easy I could hit 3s over the opposing team, only to then get in the game and actually airball. Instead, we need a humble attitude that is confident in our uniqueness, style, and abilities without tearing down or diminishing others. "You don't have to throw shade in order to shine,"

Debleaire Snell reminds us. Humility is a quality that many celebrities, athletes, and role models have, and it is a quality that sustains them because they are reminded of their finiteness. Humility looks different for each person, but it is the grounded principle of not seeing yourself higher or better than anyone else and always seeking to improve. Humility is also an attribute that sustains success. If Beyoncé thought she was perfect, she wouldn't need to practice. Instead, she constantly critiques and works tirelessly toward perfection regardless of the many compliments and awards she has received. There's a reason why some people are one-hit wonders and others are household names. A humble attitude can help catapult you once it becomes your turn to enter the game.

There are many individuals throughout history whose attitudes you can analyze before they entered the game, while they were in the game, and even after the game was completed. A person I try to model my attitude after is Jesus Christ. He was the most influential and controversial human being in history, yet He always brought the conversation back to His Father and serving those around Him. He never bragged about how many people He fed, preached in front of, or baptized. He never sought glory and recognition—once preventing a crowd from making Him King (John 6:15). Instead, He focused on His mission and embodied the qualities of patience, optimism, and humility. He knew the scriptures at the age of 12 and debated scholars who were 3 times His age, yet He disappeared or kept silent from the public light for 18 more years. When He began preaching and ministering around the age of 30, He was optimistic that the seeds and messages He would sow would produce fruit even though His own disciples doubted Him. Finally, He was humble enough to serve those around Him, even washing the feet of His disciples. Despite the traps and actions of others, He remained patient, optimistic, and humble and left an imprint on the world that outlived Him.

Remember that your attitude while you're on the bench is important in preparing, elevating, and sustaining you as you enter the arena of your life.

REFLECTIONS FROM THIS CHAPTER

Watch the Game

But be sure of this, that if the head of the house had known at what time of the night the thief was coming, he would have been on the alert and would not have allowed his house to be broken into.

—Matthew 24:43 NASB

"I don't watch basketball for entertainment. . . . For me, basketball is like reading a great book. I don't believe great books are entertainment, I think it's something that just continues to strengthen the mind. That's what I love about basketball: it continues to strengthen my mind every time I watch it."

—LeBron James

You can learn just as much watching as actually doing. As a kid, I always wanted to get my hands dirty. I wanted to be a part of whatever my eyes saw. My brother and I wanted to be mechanics for a brief moment so we destroyed our toy cars with the intention of putting them back together. We spent 3 hours smashing the toy cars on concrete and ripping the plastic covers off. After the cars were destroyed, we got distracted by our next dream—building houses, except our parents did not allow us to even touch the walls.

Getting onto the field, into the game, a relationship, finding your spouse, or starting your new idea can be fun and teach you many lessons, but watching is a great and safe teacher. You might say, "Watching is boring!!" or "I've been watching my whole life!!" but maybe you haven't been watching correctly. You see, there's a difference when you and I watch basketball and when LeBron James watches basketball. Why is that? We watch basketball for pure enjoyment and just to pass time, but LeBron, a player and competitor, watches and studies the game. He's had several instances on camera where he recalls the game and can tell you who had the ball, what play was being executed, and even the response of the defense. To LeBron, watching basketball while he was on the bench or even at home was aiding him in his understanding, and soon, the implementation of his game. Kobe Bryant, my favorite player since I was 7 years old, was a student of the sport of basketball. There are several YouTube videos that show the similarity in his game compared to Michael Jordan. How come? Because before he was in the NBA, Kobe watched MJ's games and took note of every move and situation Jordan faced. You may have been watching other people live your dream or be surrounded by friends in relationships, but the truth is you've been watching wrong. Every time you watch, you become envious or throw a pity party because you're still on the bench. Because no one asked you out on a date, no one asked you to speak, start a business, or you didn't get an invite to the NBA draft. You need to change your perspective and learn how to properly watch in order to improve your performance once in the game. The person who is courtside and the person who's in the nosebleeds can both see the game; however, the perspectives are different. You have an opportunity to watch the game on the bench or be discouraged and just watch from the stands. There's even a difference between the watcher from the bench and the watcher from the courtside seats—only one can truly impact the game. The courtside attendant can scream, jump up and down, and even pass out, yet they have no direct impact on the game. They can analyze and make suggestions, but still, their impact is small in comparison to the player on the bench. The player on the bench can eventually enter the game, execute the strategy, and enact the change they devised from watching the game.

The quote found in Matthew 24:43 is a story that Jesus told emphasizing the importance of always being alert and watching. He explains that if someone knew when their house was going to be robbed, they would stand guard at that time to prevent their possessions from being taken. Yet, the truth is, no one really knows when that moment will arrive. He admonishes His listeners to remain watchful and alert because you never know when the Son of Man will return. You're probably saying, "That's cute, but what does that have to do with me wanting to be a millionaire?" Take that same lesson that Jesus gives and replace the thief with an investor or a once-in-a-lifetime opportunity. You never really know who you will meet in an elevator or if you will be able to sell your business idea to the right person. You're rarely given a heads-up. Since you don't know when that opportunity, that special someone, or that investor may come, you need to watch the game and improve your craft until the moment arrives. If you never watched the Daytona 500 or any NASCAR race, how equipped and prepared would you be if Bubba Wallace asked you to be a part of his pit crew team? If you never watched films intently and don't understand the skill sets of the actors, writers, and directors, how prepared would you be if Shonda Rhimes, Adam Sandler, Jamie Foxx, or Viola Davis gave you an opportunity to be in their movie? Big Sean met Kanye West and was given only 16 bars to rap. If he wasn't watching intently and being prepared for that moment, would we know who he is today? The same applies for you. You have to remain alert and prepared, constantly surveying the field that you plan to enter. You have to watch for that moment that your dream can become a reality. It's time to expand and improve how you're watching from the bench.

How to Watch Correctly

It is important to watch and create an analysis of strengths, weaknesses, improvements, and environmental conditions. Imagine the arena of your life that you want to enter: sports, business, relationship, new project, acting, writing a book, and so on. While you're on the bench waiting to break through and enter, you need to do an evaluation.

- What are the strengths and benefits of being in that space/arena?
- What are the weaknesses or negatives of being in that space/arena?
- Who are individuals or organizations who've done really well in that field?
- Who can help accelerate my vision?
- What event or resource can be useful to me?
- What is lacking in that field?

- What can I bring or do differently than what is considered common?
- What is the environment like? Dynamic? Static?

These questions are really important and can help you watch correctly regardless of what area of your life that you feel stuck on the bench. These questions can help frame how you approach the field that you're seeking to enter and provide guidance on how to execute your dreams and vision.

Let's take an example of you deciding to enter a relationship or even a marriage. It would be wise to take an inventory of the relationships and marriages you see around you, starting with your parents, family, neighbors, church, social spheres, and so on. Once you've identified a wide case study, begin to analyze and decipher the strengths and benefits of being married. What do couples say is a benefit? What do you see as a benefit? Are those benefits worth it for you to pursue? Next, what are the negatives, costs, or frustrations of being married? What are the main sources of problems, arguments, and even divorce? Knowing this information can assist you with the future problems you will have to solve and work through. Who are some role models that have a healthy, progressing marriage? How did they do it? Learning their story and understanding their experience can better condition and equip you before you enter. Finally, ask yourself—what do you expect from a relationship, and can you provide what you expect as well? You can apply all of these questions and modes of thinking to whatever field, idea, project, or arena that you want to enter. You have to begin to watch in such a way that prepares you for the moment the coach points at you and says, "You're in!"

One day I was on the bench and we were getting whooped. I wasn't really paying attention to the game and was mostly thinking of which cheerleader would be nice enough to sit by me at lunch. I finally had my eye set on the one I was going to ask until someone grabbed my jersey and lifted me to my feet. "Grand-Jean!! Replace Bobby and don't do what he's doing!!" I was so happy and excited for the chance to finally get in the game and impress the cheerleaders. We lined up on the court for the free throw. "Ammishaddai!!" said my teammate. "Make sure to get Bobby's man!!"

Our opponents missed the free throw, but regained possession. I looked around frantically trying to find the person I was supposed to guard. "He's over there!! He's on the three line!!" my teammates on the bench yelled. The opposite team was running some play and everyone seemed to be just a blur. I was lost and was going to just pick someone to guard or double team until I saw one player open. He had possession of the ball and I ran toward him to block him. I jumped in the air as he rose with the ball. *Narrator: "It was at that moment that Ammishaddai knew he messed up."* I was too late. My opponent had plenty of time to shoot, and he drained a 3 while I was still in the air. I came crashing down on the floor and scuffed my knees. The crowd went wild. "Time-out, ref!! Grand-Jean, you're out!!" My teammates made fun of me and the cheerleaders were all laughing. I'd been watching the game, but my mind was really somewhere else. If I had been intentional to understand who was covering who and what weaknesses the opposite team had, I could've made an impact on the game. My pride and body were hurt, but most importantly, I ruined my time in the game because I had failed to watch.

Are you not being intentional watching the arena that you want to enter? What if you cut short your time off the bench because you made the same mistake that you could've avoided if you were just paying attention? It's time to start asking questions and being intentional. Ask your parents about the mistakes they've made and what they would have done differently. Watch comedy skits and see the patterns in how successful comedians woo their audience. Analyze the delivery and vocabulary of President Barack Obama's speech until you remember it like your favorite song. Read a diverse amount of autobiographies of successful business owners and study their dark chapters and how they overcame. Next time, don't just watch a movie, but take time to notice and appreciate the changes in scenes, plot, suspense, and climax. Begin to use your time on the bench to watch and learn from those who came before you and those who are playing right now so that you will have the best and longest tenure in the game. You don't want to get divorced 3 months after getting married over something you would have avoided completely if you had spent more time observing your partner. You don't want to finally get that business deal or that opportunity to open up for a major artist and ruin it only because you weren't watching and adjusting your craft accordingly.

COMPARISON

It's extremely important to mention that your "watching" of the game should not become a comparison that feeds envy, insecurity, and doubt. We live in a world that encourages us to compare ourselves to everyone around us. Social media has been a large vehicle of comparison lately. You open up Instagram and see that your friend is on vacation in Jamaica in the middle of a pandemic while you're at home being yelled at by your parents. You open up Twitter and your other friend has a high-paying job with benefits while your inbox keeps saying "we regret to inform you." You open up Facebook and your other friend got accepted to medical school while you sent 30 applications and haven't heard back yet. Of course, you like the image, tweet, and leave a nice comment, but deep in your heart, feelings of envy and disappointment begin to take root because you ask yourself,

"Why not me? Why aren't things working out for me? Why am I still stuck while everyone is living their best life?" I don't want to call you out because we all have been there, and most of us are still there. Everyone on social media, including me sometimes, only high-lights the good parts of their life. Rarely do you see a video or picture of someone crying, looking rough, talking about their struggles, or that they tried to harm themselves today. We have bought into this system where we airbrush the reality and flaws of our lives, and only accentuate praiseworthy moments. As a result, we assume that life is going well for everyone else except us. We feel that if we don't have any news or exciting thing to share, we should just keep quiet and watch everyone else. There's a balance between watching to take notes and improve your skill set versus comparing and complaining that you're not like so and so or that you wish you had the gift of gab, that body, talent, or that you were a born genius. Comparison steals, robs, and sows seeds of discon-tentment that eventually kill the gifts you were given. We are constantly looking at others and daydreaming about how we desire to be in that role only to miss out on the gold mine that is beneath us if we would simply take time to dig and work on ourselves. We desire the mountaintop moments but reject the valley experiences that lead us to the mountaintop! I'm preaching if you haven't noticed already.

When I was in the fourth grade, there was this student named Jimmy who loved to finish his test first. His nose was always in the air and he would always adjust his glasses as he answered all of the teacher's questions. He would refer to me by my last name only for some reason. "Hello, Grand-Jean. Was that question a little challenging for you?" he'd say sarcastically. As a natural nerd, I felt challenged by his intelligence and so I wanted to show him that he wasn't the only genius in our class. Every test day we would rush through our questions to see who would be the first to turn in our exam. We would rush out of our seats and begin shoving each other so we could be the first to turn in our exam. Until one day when the teacher requested a meeting with my father. "Ammishaddai has been comparing and competing with a certain student in our class. The difference is that the student has received As on his assignments while your son is currently at a C average," the teacher said politely. "Sir? Are you OK?" she asked with concern as she watched my father's face transform and burn with anger. "I am OK. My son, however, is not OK," my father replied as he began taking off his belt. That was the last time I compared myself to my classmate.

Many of us are comparing ourselves to others, and as a result, we've modified our uniqueness and sped up our process in a disingenuous attempt to emulate our perceived competition. However, we are disappointed and even more frustrated when it doesn't work for us. You will be just like me sitting at a C average trying to compare and compete with everyone else. You should be intentional in watching and learning from others while appreciating the beauty, uniqueness, and process of your journey. You will get off of the bench eventually, but comparison will only prolong your time on the bench and shorten your time in the game.

There's a biblical quote I love that says, "Suppose one of you wants to build a tower. Won't you first sit down and estimate the cost to see if you have enough money to complete it? For if you lay the foundation and are not able to finish it, everyone who sees it will ridicule you, saying, 'This person began to build and wasn't able to finish'" (Luke 14:28–30 NIV). This quote always convicts me because it reminds me of the importance of watching and planning before you engage in anything. It's so easy for us to just jump in, and often we are encouraged to do so; however, there are more risks than benefits if we enter an area that we are unfamiliar with or have poorly watched. Counting the costs, asking for advice, and seeking mentors are just some of the few things that will make a difference in your performance once it's your time to enter the game. You don't want to be a one-hit wonder or be a topic of embarrassment because you weren't a student of the game before you tried to be a master.

Everyone wants instant success, and sometimes it happens, but the pattern behind every long-tenure success in any field is that the individual who achieves it first watched consistently and worked to improve their craft. I wish I could tell you that watching and learning stops once you actually get in the game and begin your career and dream, but that would be a lie.

I personally don't love school even though I have two certificates, two bachelor degrees, and a master's. Learning is like breathing. With every new source of information and knowledge you receive, you're breathing life into your career, dreams, and passions. If you think you've learned enough, it's like holding your breath and still conducting all your activities. Eventually, your lungs will burst and your dream will die. You don't have to get a degree or go to college, but you must strive to be a lifelong student—learning from mentors, competitors, and even from yourself. LeBron James is an accomplished athlete and is set for life, but he remains a student of basketball, constantly watching tapes and games despite his busy schedule. Beyoncé will forever be a memorable and impactful artist, yet she continues to critique her performances and improves with every new project. If you would like to last long in the field that you're attempting to enter, watch the game. Watch the game while you're still on the bench, because when you're in the actual game, it is difficult to see everything that you saw when you were on the bench. It becomes harder to see the weaknesses and the areas that need improvement.

If you begin to watch intently now, then you'll save yourself time and effort and reap a sustained and successful career.

Reflections from This Chapter

Strategize

"If any of you lacks wisdom, let him ask God, who gives to all generously and without reproach, and it will be given to him."
—James 1:5 NASB

"Strategy is about setting yourself apart from the competition. It's not a matter of being better at what you do—it's a matter of being different at what you do."
—Michael Porter

You finally have your attitude in the right positive space and you've improved how you watch the game and arena you're desiring to enter. The next step is to take the information and answers you received from watching and develop a strategy. A strategy is a game plan of how you're going to achieve your dream and vision. What are the steps you are going to take in order to reach that goal? What is your business plan? How are you going to go on tour? How are you going to make it to the NBA draft? How are you going to get on Broadway or receive that Dove award? Your strategy looks different depending on the field, but the common thread is that it serves as the vehicle toward your destination.

Developing a strategy is easy, but developing a strategy that is *effective* requires skill. Almost everyone has a strategy. Some people unknowingly have a strategy to lose or even to stay on the bench forever. It's similar to the phrase "Failure to plan is planning to fail." You have to be intentional with the strategy you develop and ensure you pull from the wisdom you gained from viewing your environment. Many people like to say, "I'm just going with the flow." Although that sounds good, you're missing out on many things that you could achieve and attain if you'd just set some time aside and make a plan and a strategy. It's time for you to analyze the strategy you have and build upon it with the information you gathered from watching the game.

I love playing board games because of the fun and competitive spirit that they invoke. Among all board games, I love Monopoly and chess the most. Neither game requires physical skill aside from moving a piece or reading a card, but they involve intense strategy. If you begin the game simply thinking you're going to win by doing one move or by not losing all your money, then you have already lost. While the object of the game is simple, there are many barriers and even opponents that intend to cause you to lose. Your strategy has to be able to survive in uncertain circumstances and in an environment that is controlled by chance. Both games require a strategy that is solid, complete, malleable, and effective. These fundamental characteristics are common among winning strategies regardless of the field or arena you intend to enter. Let's briefly discuss what they look like in practice.

A strategy must be solid and complete. It sounds simple, but most strategies that people come up with lack preparation and wisdom, and aren't complete. They begin the strategy without knowing what to do next.

In college, I had a huge crush on this smart, outgoing, and beautiful girl, and so I wanted to ask her to go out with me. She definitely could make your heart stop and cause you to lose your train of thought, so you had to come prepared. I was much smoother than I'd been in high school; I had confidence and swag, and my strategy was simple: ask her out on a date. My heart was beating fast, my armpits were itchy, and my mouth was dry. "H-Hey, beautiful, my name is Ammishaddai, but you can call me Big Mish." (I told you I was smooth.) She began to laugh and blush; I knew that I had her hooked. It was time for me to bring out the big guns and execute my strategy. "So I was wondering if you'd like to go out with me sometime when you're available." "I'd love to!" I was so shocked that she said yes. I started envisioning our wedding day and then our honeymoon and the names of our kids. (Yea, I was that type of guy.) I was already typing the Instagram caption that I would use to make all the high-school girls jealous until she finally got my attention. "Earth to Big Mish! You there?" "O-Oh, yea, yea, I'm here." "For the third time, when and where would you like to go?" "When and where??" I started repeating the question as if she were speaking ancient Greek. The truth is, I didn't think I was going to get this far. I had the confidence, swag, and strategy, but my strategy didn't consist of where and when we would go out. I was just trying to have her say yes and start bragging to my friends. "I . . . I, uh, let me check my calendar and get back to you—can I get your number?" I said as smoothly as possible. "You can get my number when you know when and where we're going on a date. Bye, Big Mish," she said as she walked away with my jaw and heart in her hand. I mean, can you believe the audacity?! Now, I'm sure you're just as shocked as I am or probably laughing at my pain, but she taught me a very valuable and memorable lesson. You see, my strategy was simple: ask her out on a date. Yet, my strategy was not complete or solid. I did not think of a day, time, and location in case she said yes and inquired. She had every right to ask me and I should have been prepared with at least 2 options. Many of us do and say the same thing: "I didn't think I was going to get that far!" Unfortunately, we doubt ourselves and develop an incomplete strategy that causes us to lose the game and prize.

When you develop a strategy, it needs to be complete from start to finish. You need to imagine every possibility and have a contingency plan. If you go into a game expecting to lose or not expecting to even place, you've impaired your performance. "For as he thinketh in his heart, so is he" (Proverbs 23:7 KJV). If you think you're not going to be influential in your arena or you think that the coach won't ever put you in the game, then once you're actually in the game and are a major influencer, you won't know how to act or what to do. This is why there are so many one-hit wonders. They did not create a sustainable strategy. They just wanted to become famous and rich, and once they arrived, they didn't know what else to do or have a continuous plan. Your strategy should be similar to a plate. It should be able to hold the food that is placed on it. A complete strategy holds the food, regardless of how high it may be. Yet, an incomplete strategy is like trying to eat soup with a bowl that has holes in it. Whatever blessing you receive will slip through due to your incomplete strategy. When I finally had a complete strategy, I asked that beautiful girl out with a date, time, location, attire, and even told her the forecast. She was flattered, but told me that she was seriously dating someone else. Don't be like me. Develop a solid and complete strategy. Hey, Siri, play "Marvins Room" by Drake.

The next important characteristic of a great strategy is its malleability. *Malleable* means that the substance can be changed, altered, or influenced. This is important because of the unknown events of life that can and will occur. If life would go as planned, then we would all know what to do and not suffer as much as we do now; however, there is the occasional "life" that occurs or events that we don't see coming. There are several examples of this that you have probably experienced. These events can attack your strategy, your emotion, your headspace, confidence, and even your body. For example, you've decided to become a professional basketball player and your strategy is to work out and be in the best shape physically and mentally to achieve your goals of playing in front of thousands of fans. After securing your athletic scholarship, you tear your Achilles tendon. You definitely didn't expect that and didn't see it coming. Can you still play professional basketball? Of course you can, but not with the same strategy. You probably have to increase your efforts in areas such as conditioning, working out, and shooting off of one leg like Kobe. Now, that might be an extreme example, but you have to have a strategy that can be malleable. You can alter or make changes as you move ahead. The same thing is evident in chess. Your strategy is to place your opponent in checkmate and end the game. On your way to accomplish that strategy, your queen, the most powerful piece, is captured. It's easy to fret or give up, thinking the game is lost, but you have to be able to change and alter your strategy. You can still win the game and capture your opponent without the queen; you just have to adjust your strategy.

Having a malleable strategy is so important because typically people go through life with only one mindset, and when an unexpected issue arises, they freak out or they believe that the same strategy will be sufficient to bring them to their end goal. It's as simple as wanting to make all As in school. When you were in high school, you studied an hour a day and got all As. Now you're in college and studying an hour a day gets you Bs and Cs. Your strategy has been to study an hour a day and you've kept that strategy despite the natural changes of new arenas and levels. If you've made your strategy stagnant and consistent—always studying for 1 hour—you'll continue to decline until you won't reach your goal. Instead, you need to realize that you are in a new and more complex environment that is going to require your strategy to improve and grow. It's a simple concept, but many people are in love with familiarity and "that's the way we've always done it!" but we all know the definition of insanity—"doing the same thing and expecting different results." Changing and improving your strategy based on new information and events is vital to having a winning strategy.

In 1992, Arkansas governor Bill Clinton was running for president of the United States. Amongst a crowded primary, his last stand occurred in New Hampshire. He was polling low and the media said he should drop out of the race. His strategy leading up to the New Hampshire primary had been to do press conferences and talk to the media—until he brought in state campaign experts and asked them for their honest feedback. They responded with a simple and new strategy: stop doing press conferences and talking to the media and start talking to the people and shake every hand. They believed that his personality and charisma would have a special effect with voters. He altered his strategy and began to have more interaction with voters. New Hampshire marked the moment where his campaign began to grow and rapidly spread until he reached the White House. His humble and sincere desire to change his approach in order to achieve his intended outcome is one of the many examples of the benefits of having a malleable strategy.

Lastly, it is important for your strategy to be effective. This simply means that the strategy works and brings out the best outcome for you in your desired field. Most simple games and scenarios have a dominant strategy. The infamous Prisoner's Dilemma, created by Albert Tucker, is a scenario where a prisoner has to make a decision that could possibly lead to 4 outcomes. For example, if the prisoner confesses and his accomplice confesses, they both receive 5 years. If the prisoner confesses and his accomplice doesn't confess, then the prisoner serves 2 years and the accomplice receives 10 years. Vice versa if the prisoner doesn't confess and the accomplice confesses. If both the prisoner and accomplice don't confess, they are both free. In this matrix decision, the best choice, or most logical one, is for *both* prisoners not to confess. (Snitches get stitches, right?!) That is considered the dominant or most effective strategy. However, the prisoners are separated and don't have the opportunity to know the intentions or decisions of the other. As a result, the prisoner must make a choice considering the best outcome for him in the midst of uncertainty.

We all have a similarly tough decision to make. Your decision has costs and benefits, and you have to create the most effective strategy in the midst of other people pursuing strategies that can affect your outcome. An effective strategy considers the factors and uncertainties of the environment and makes the best decision. An effective strategy to get into the college of your choice is to always study. Regardless of other factors, continuous study brings you a greater chance for your test scores and grades to improve. The same goes for music, acting, and sports. The effective strategy shows you that if you remain consistent in practice and preparation you will reap the benefits. An ineffective strategy is not consistent and is spotty. It's like saying some weeks I'll work and some weeks I won't as you're trying out for the Olympics. An effective strategy realizes that there may be interruptions, life events, and even unexpected barriers, but controlling what you can control and remaining consistent brings your vision closer to reality.

DON'T FORGET TO LAND

When formulating a solid, malleable, and effective strategy, it's important to begin with the end in mind. Many of us think about just getting there or arriving at our desired destination, but we must remember that we cannot remain there forever. If it's not term limits, it's health and aging that will humble you and remind you that you cannot stay forever. Actors, athletes, preachers, artists, chefs, and whatever profession you can imagine has a finite time because we are finite beings. We all have a date with destiny that is inescapable. Planes have strategies to get in the air and to remain in the air; however, the resources of the plane are finite and eventually the plane has to come down and land. This is why all the uncertainty and characteristics of the forecast and environment are incorporated in the pilot's plan in order to ensure a proper and safe landing. Your strategy has to include how you will land the plane and keep yourself intact. Some planes go up whole and come down tarnished or disfigured. As a result, you have to create the final component of your master plan—your exit strategy.

Nipsey Hussle, a rapper, activist, and entrepreneur, once said, "I got an album concept called *Exit Strategy* that might be one of my last ones. It's a term they use in business when you build companies. You create an exit strategy as you make a company. You don't wait till you're five years in it; you create an exit strategy as you make the company."

An exit strategy is the final component of your plan to get off the bench. You need to have the faith and belief that you will get off of the bench and be a major player in your desired field, and one day you will retire, sell the business, or transition into being a coach or mentor. You need to take time while you're on the bench to plan your landing, your final monologue, your last dance. This is why many athletes go on to coach or become commentators, why politicians become professors and educators, and why artists and musicians become producers. An exit strategy ensures that you arrive and end at your desired destination and that you know where you want to go after the buzzer goes off.

"Write the vision and make it plain on tablets, that he may run who reads it (Habakkuk 2:2 NKJV). It's important to write your vision and then write your strategy on how you're going to attain and reach that goal. What steps are you going to take once you're in the arena of your life? How will you sustain yourself and your dream? What does retirement look like? In order to answer these questions, your strategy needs to be complete, with no holes. Plan from beginning until end. Malleable, you can change and alter your strategy depending on the uncertainties of life. Finally, an effective strategy is one that consists of a dominant plan, which, when implemented, will allow you to reap the optimal benefits. This is easy to read, but hard to put into action. That is why James 1:5 reminds us that God is able and willing to give us wisdom if we simply ask for it. He will show you and tell you what to do if you take the time to ask, watch, and plan. You're almost ready to get off the bench, but take the necessary time to strategize before you go in.

TAKING RISKS

A time will always present itself when you must take a risk. At times you'll have to choose between right and right or wrong and wrong. Every decision you make has some type of uncertainty built in, and it is very rare to pursue a dream or career and not experience some sort of risk. The first thing to note is that risks aren't bad at all. It is in the moments where we experience risks that we are able to build and expand our faith. Second Corinthians 5:7 (NIV) reminds us, "For we live by faith, not by sight." Whether you realize it or not, you are utilizing faith when you make a decision. Whether you decide to drive yourself or take public transportation, both of these decisions have risks. So, what do you do when you find yourself in a decision where both risks are high? It is important to go back to your strategy. Your strategy should always point you back toward your overall goal and dream that you want to reach. This will then guide you toward the best decision to make even though there are risks on both sides. You should not take risks just because there is a potential high reward, but because they will aid you in reaching your goal quicker or more safely. My mentor often referred to this as pursuing "judicious risks." Judicious risks are risks that you engage in and take on after using wise and prudent judgment and when you align your decision with prayer, morals, values, and common sense. Your judicious risk may not be the same as mine because we have different values and goals, but you must practice making the best decision regardless of the risks.

Imagine you are a 4.0 student, and in your last semester you are required to choose between Econometrics and Paleo-Archaic History. The Econometrics professor is known for tanking students' GPAs due to the rigorous coursework and tests, but if you pass the class, companies are promising to hire you and start you at $85,000. The Paleo-Archaic History professor is known for being really engaging, straightforward, and most students get an A in the class. Your dream was to be valedictorian of your class and to be recognized and honored in front of tens of thousands at your graduation. If you take the Econometrics class, more than likely you'll make a B, thus dropping your GPA and missing out on being valedictorian. If you take Paleo-Archaic History, you'll get an A and become valedictorian, but have a job with a starting salary of only $50,000. This is a made-up example, of course, but it mimics the weird and frustrating decisions we are often confronted with. I will let you decide what you should do, but in a decision where you have pros and cons on both sides, it is important to remember what your strategy is. What is your end goal? What do you value? What decision would you be OK with if it were your last? We all need to practice taking judicious risks, and the answer often lies within a well-formulated strategy.

DISCIPLINE

Finally, in order to cement and make a strategy effective, you must develop discipline. Discipline, in regard to strategy, is when you stick to your goal and make the necessary and undeviating actions in order to attain it. To be honest, discipline is annoying and not always comfortable or pleasant, but it garners the greatest rewards if you remain consistent and steadfast. Hebrews 12:11 (NIV) states, "No discipline seems pleasant at the time, but painful. Later on, however, it produces a harvest of righteousness and peace for those who have been trained by it." One reason that many people never achieve their ambitions and desired goals is because they lack discipline. Discipline is waking up every day at 6:00 am in order to have enough time before the day starts to write that book or train for that marathon. Discipline is reading a new book every month, sticking to a schedule, or being the first one at practice and the last one to leave. It's through discipline that we know the names of great athletes, chefs, movie producers, doctors, and so forth. You've probably heard the saying "Everybody wanna shine, but nobody wanna grind!" Everyone wants to have billions in their bank accounts and their name and face in a magazine, but no one wants to put in the unchanging grunt work in order to achieve and maintain that status. Discipline will take you toward your dreams quicker and keep you there longer. What parts of your life need a consistent dose of discipline?

REFLECTIONS FROM THIS CHAPTER

_____

_____

_____

_____

_____

_____

_____

_____

_____

_____

_____

_____

_____

Practice

*"But don't just listen to God's word. You must
do what it says. Otherwise, you are only
fooling yourselves."*
—James 1:22–23 NLT

*"It's what you practice in private that you will
be rewarded for in public."*
—Anthony Robbins

In 2002, a basketball player sat during a press
conference and gave a rant that would forever be
memorialized in the minds of the sports world.

"We sitting in here—I'm supposed to be the franchise player, and we in here talking about practice. I mean, listen: we talking about practice. Not a game. Not a game. We talking about practice. Not a game. Not the game that I go out there and die for and play every game like it's my last. Not the game. We talking about practice, man"

Allen Iverson, arguably, was one of the most talented, gifted, and memorable point guards in the NBA. Averaging more than 25 points per game and an 11-time NBA All Star, he captivated the crowd with his special moves and passes. Yet, despite his stats and swagger, he never won an NBA Championship. His statement is similar to many of our perceptions of practice. It's annoying and inconvenient. We want to get into the game and be the one making decisions and involved in the action. Yet, because we do not warm up and practice, we do not reach our complete potential. (To be fair, Allen Iverson had issues going on in his personal life and said it influenced his statement that day.)

Once you possess the correct attitude, watch the arena correctly, and strategize a plan that will sustain and make you successful, it's time to put words into action. While you may not be in the actual game, on tour, in your dream career, or marriage, you can still warm up. You can still practice the strategies and the footage you've collected from being on the bench.

We often receive a period of time right before we enter into the arena to be able to warm up and practice. You often see basketball players and athletes warming up and practicing their shots, swings, and techniques. In those moments, it's not rigorous because they are saving their energy for the actual match. Yet, the true practice occurs days, weeks, and even years before the moment. Simone Biles is a decorated Olympian and has won gold several times in her field, yet the Olympics only occur once every 4 years. It is arguably the most challenging event, because you only get that one moment to prove yourself and attain the prize. That is why she spends long hours daily to prepare her mind and body for an event that comes just twice a decade.

One day in college, I was trying to spit game at a young shawty, and as we were walking, we ran into a lounge that had a piano. "Do you play?" she said, motioning at the piano. Her eyes were captivating and her smile made my heart skip 2 beats. "Of course I can. Girl, do you know I'm the black Beethoven!?" I said as I raced toward the piano. I enjoy playing the piano and was fortunate to take lessons growing up.

I played countless pieces, and one of my favorites is a selection from Beethoven. It's my go-to song when I'm trying to impress a girl. She stood in front of the piano flashing that smile and I shot one back as I positioned my fingers on the keys. Her captivating image soon began to deteriorate until it appeared as if her face was having a seizure and she began to cover her ears. I was about to call 911 until she said, "What in the world was that!?" She had no mercy in her rebuke and roasting of my skills. While she may have exaggerated my poor performance, she was right; I hadn't touched the piano in almost a year. I lacked the consistency factor in my practice so that, when the moment finally arrived, I missed it completely. We ended up no longer talking; her loss, though, am I right? When your practice becomes consistent, you're able to improve and retain your skills.

It's important for you to begin to practice your craft. No more complaining about being on the bench and feeling as if you've been there forever. Instead, change your attitude and mindset and see it as an opportunity for you to practice the things you're going to do once you're in the arena. If you want to become a filmmaker, then this is the time to practice your script writing, directing, and production. Continue to produce short films and gather feedback from those around you. If you desire to be a chef at a major establishment in town, this is your time to practice your craft and build upon the knowledge you've gained. It's time for you to stand in front of the mirror and recite those lines as if you're auditioning at The Juilliard School.

My 8th-grade coach made decisions on who entered the game based on their performance during practice. We didn't really take practice seriously because there were no cheerleaders or screaming fans. We just ran the drills to get them over with. Yet, once the actual game started, we played with excitement and frenzy, but forgot the plays and techniques from practice. We spent time fixing our mindset, watching footage, and strategizing, but because we didn't take practice seriously, our performance was poor. Practice separates the good from the great.

Kobe Bryant was notoriously known for his extreme and consistent practice routine. He would be the first one at practice, already getting a full workout

3 hours before the official practice began. He would practice with a cast on his arm or finger and force his teammates to stay after practice to try new moves on them. When training for the Olympics, he held practice from 4:15 am to 11:00 am and wouldn't leave until he took 800 shots. Kobe Bryant had an unmatched love for the sport of basketball and it showed in his work ethic and results. As a result, he played for 20 seasons, was an 18-time All Star, 5-time NBA World Champion, and 2-time NBA Finals MVP. He had a decorated career and was a major influence to several generations. The closest I ever got to Kobe Bryant was shaking hands and taking a picture with Dwayne Wade (another favorite player of mine). The day that Kobe went to rest with his ancestors, the world stopped. It was shocking and still hard to believe because he had an invincible persona and such an incredible and special impact on everyone he came into contact with.

An NBA scout said in 2008, "Allen Iverson loves to play when the lights come on. Kobe loves doing the s--- before the lights come on." Allen Iverson had unquestionable talent and skill that came naturally. He didn't need to practice and was still better than most players. I believe that Kobe Bryant was less talented than many notable basketball legends, but his work ethic surpassed them all. He was the hardest-working athlete of our generation. His consistency and commitment to practice elevated him above many players who may have had better skills or talent because he remained disciplined and motivated. We can only imagine and argue what type of player Allen Iverson would be if he had just half of Kobe's work ethic. The difference is evident in the accolades Kobe received compared to Allen. We, too, can find ourselves in similar boats. Some people are naturally talented and gifted in whatever field they choose. They just have that natural ability to learn languages, speak well, sing, act, dance, play multiple sports, or be a master chess player. Others have been blessed with a deep desire and disciplined commitment toward a field, and as a result they strive daily to perfect their craft. Unfortunately, gifted people can become so comfortable in their natural talents that they do not develop them and build upon them. Instead, they settle for mediocrity, while those who have a stellar and unchanging work ethic achieve great and unimaginable heights. It is important to take the information and knowledge you have received and practice before you get into the game. The choice is yours. Either you'll be an Allen Iverson or a Kobe Bryant.

Many times, our eyes stray toward the reward. We want to receive that wedding ring, the title, position, Oscar, championship, or financial level, yet we forget that it is practice that makes us qualified to reach such heights. Our generation, thanks to social media, has become obsessed with being in front of a camera. We televise and share every part of our lives to the world. The truth is that social media grants us a glimpse of a life of fame and power.

We want to be in the spotlight, have our face on *TIME* magazine, and see our names in shining lights. We often chase the benefits but run away from the work that is required to arrive at such levels. Tony Robbins said it best: "It's what you practice in private that you will be rewarded for in public." You have to learn to be comfortable practicing in private. You have to learn to be comfortable working hard and staying consistent when no one is watching. When the camera is off, when no one is in the stands, when no one is tuned in to your Instagram/Facebook live, practice as if the world is watching. Practice until it becomes second nature that you can recite that song in your sleep, that you can dribble with your eyes closed and with your opposite hand, that you can do it backwards. I enjoy giving motivational talks and sermons, and one day I noticed my mentor gave them without any notes. Not once could you see him use a piece of paper. He later told me that he practiced and memorized his sermons so much that they were in his mind and he could deliver them with ease and be free to captivate and uplift the crowd. It was a daunting feat, but with practice and consistency, I was able to experience the freedom from pen and paper. It's amazing to imagine all of the new skills and comfort you can build from making practice a routine and a habit.

It's easy to hear these words and the examples of the benefits of practicing and warming up before you enter, but it can be challenging or intimidating to implement them. The following verse from James always convicts me because it is something that I struggle with daily. "But don't just listen to God's word. You must do what it says. Otherwise, you are only fooling yourselves. For if you listen to the word and don't obey, it is like glancing at your face in a mirror. You see yourself, walk away, and forget what you look like" (James 1:22–24 NLT). We do this with many things. We read an inspiring and captivating book, like this one:), listen to or watch a motivating speech, but we go back to doubting ourselves and continuing our unhealthy habits. We glance in the mirror and see what we need to do, but we go away and make no necessary changes to achieve our desired image. Start practicing the suggestions in this book. Start practicing your craft and talent. Surround yourself with people who are just as hungry and determined as you are to achieve that next level. Have accountability partners to keep you consistent with your regimen. It's common sense, but a rare practice. We all know what to do, but when it comes to putting it together, we hesitate and put it off.

Many times, while writing this book, I stepped away or had writer's block and didn't want to continue. Writing a book while you're unemployed in the heat of a pandemic doesn't make it easier, but I had to remember that I know this book will be helpful to that one person who is transitioning from the bench to the arena. That one person waiting for their time to enter into their destiny. It may be annoying or appear as a lost cause at times, but just the thought of that one person seeing their life transform made the process worth it. So, every day, I had to practice praying, speaking positive words of affirmation, and writing despite my moods or my external environment. I'm thankful to God for being able to publish this book, because regardless, it remains a testament to its lessons coming to life. It could not be possible until I stopped just reading, hearing, and talking about it and actually practiced it when no one was watching.

Remember that practice is more about discipline and consistency. Motivation comes and goes and is too volatile to rely on. External factors can easily sink motivation, but discipline maintains performance, and consistency forms skill. Once you are able to create a disciplined practice routine, you are able to develop yourself as you become an expert in your field. We are often closer to our desired destination than we can imagine, and all that stands in our way is practicing the words and lessons we know to be true. True practice doesn't make, find, or settle for excuses. If it's raining, then train inside. If you don't have an important piece of equipment, then find a substitute or make it work without it. If you ever feel like you have a valid excuse on why you can't practice and perfect your vision and dream, then please remember, "Excuses are tools of the incompetent to build bridges to nowhere and monuments of nothingness." Get up and get to work.

REFLECTIONS FROM THIS CHAPTER

_____

_____

_____

_____

_____

_____

_____

_____

_____

_____

_____

_____

_____

Don't Go in before You're Called

"See how the farmer waits for the land to yield its valuable crop, patiently waiting for the autumn and spring rains. You too, be patient and stand firm."

—James 5:7–8 NIV

"I know shortcuts cut short long runs."

—Chance the Rapper

One of my favorite sports growing up before basketball was Jump Rope/Double Dutch. When I was younger, I really didn't have cable consistently 'cause it was expensive, and the basic television could only do so much. So my siblings, my cousins, and I spent most of our time outside using our imagination and playing competitive games. My cousin took a piece of rope and tied it from one end and gave me the other end. She then told me to swing the rope in a circular motion as fast as I could. As I enjoyed seeing the rope go in circles, I was quickly startled when I saw my cousin dart toward it. "Don't stop turning it!" she yelled as tears swelled my eyes due to the fear that I would hurt her. (I was only 8.) Seemingly without hesitation, she jumped into the circular rope and began to stay in it, appearing to almost levitate with ease. I let go of the rope, crying as I ran looking for garlic and fire thinking she was a witch. (We were learning about the Salem Witch Trials in school.) Once she assured me that she wasn't a witch, I begged her to teach me the ways of levitating in the circular (aka jump) rope.

We then began to practice for hours, but no matter how hard I tried, I could never imitate what she did. I was frustrated and began to head back inside filled with rope burns and bruises. "Try it one last time, but remember, don't go in before you're called!" my cousin said to me. She then began the crazy orbiting contraption and all I could think of was jumping inside without getting hurt or disturbing the systemic flow. "Now!" she yelled as I closed my eyes and ran toward the jump rope and prepared for my final beatdown. To my surprise, the rope continued to go in its circular motion and I was unharmed. I leaped for joy until my cousin's arm was tired. I walked away feeling like a champion ... and a wizard.

You see, the dream career or goal you envision is very similar to jumping rope. The rope is already in motion and it is intimidating to just jump in. You see those you admire who seem to enter and remain in the circular motion rope with ease. So you decide to join them and make a name for yourself, but every time you try to join, you get hit, discouraged, or the rope stops turning. Many of us face this same dilemma in various areas of life. You feel like you can never make it past the first date. No one is buying your products even though you're black owned. Your granny thinks you're funny, but you can't get a gig. You've memorized a whole script to a movie, but can't star in a show. We all aspire and dare to get off the bench and jump into the game, make the winning shot, and have our names hung in the arena forever. Yet we need to master how to get into the game. The answer is not some secret but a notorious, rare, and difficult task that grants bountiful riches and heart's desires. The key to actually getting into the game is, "Don't go in until you're called."

I hate being patient. It is frustrating, boring, unpleasant, and annoying. Why do good things come to those who wait? Why can't they come swiftly? Patience is widely known yet rarely seen in action. We desire to skip the process of waiting for the right moment, because we want to decide when. We want to instantly be the CEO, the #1 rapper, the face of Nollywood or Bollywood, governor of our state, or president of the country. Yet, our lack of patience is what holds us back from entering that arena or achieving our desired outcome. We have the right attitude, we've watched and noticed the patterns, we've developed a strategic plan to enter, and we've stretched and practiced, but the last step is patience. All the knowledge and preparation in the world still cannot grant you what patience gives. It takes patience to realize that there is a cycle, and while you may want to be in the game right now making decisions, it may not be your time. It is a very mature and hard lesson to understand and accept. Most elevations and promotions are centered around timing. It's almost as if that person or invention was made for the moment. You can have the talent and the resources to be successful and achieve your dreams, but timing your launch perfectly is what really makes you soar.

The Wright brothers were attempting to achieve the impossible by defying the law of gravity. They built the correct contraption and had the right tools and resources necessary to put a plane into the sky, but before they began their flight, it was all about timing. They had to ensure that the weather was cooperative and that the wind was blowing at the perfect speed in order to set their plane in motion. It's hard at times to place a finger or to truly know when, but I believe that the moment speaks to you. It stirs your soul in such a way that you know it's your time. As if you're being called. The truth is that many of us try to enter into different fields before we're called. We rush into marriage, business contracts, or pursue degrees just to make our parents happy or have letters next to our name. Many people actually get into the game and their desired destination, but don't last long or find themselves miserable because they entered before they were called.

This science or philosophy applies to many areas of life. Imagine if the sun came out too early, or if a butterfly emerged from its cocoon too soon, or fall came in July, or if you bit into a pie that had just come out of the oven. All of these situations would cause drastic effects if they were real (especially your tongue after biting into that hot pie). Lao Tzu once said, "Nature does not hurry, yet everything is accomplished." We have bought into this false notion that we need to be quick or we'll lose our moment and opportunity. If we don't get married at 25 then we'll never find someone, or if we don't become a millionaire in our 20s then we'll never be successful. These are falsehoods that we've repeated and believed, and as a result we've made rash decisions that have caused us pain and regret. If you simply ask your parents or any elder, "What did you do out of haste that you wish you'd waited for? What are you glad that you waited for?" then you'll have to carry some tissue and hear the often sad and painful stories that you wouldn't even imagine. The Chinese proverb is right: "One moment of patience may ward off great disaster. One moment of impatience may ruin a whole life." It's important for us to hold control of our desires and passions to be in the game and gain wisdom by patiently waiting for the right time to enter. Next time you're faced with making a decision, breathe, pray, and seek counsel. In that moment, it can seem miniscule, but the effects can be long lasting. If you truly desire to be successful and enter into your arena, then seek patience, which propels you and makes your feet firm.

Ecclesiastes reminds us that there is a time for everything. There are seasons of our lives that guide our growth and maturation. Just as the mango tree cannot push forth in December no matter how dire its desire is, so we cannot force our entry into certain seasons just because our passion is high. Again, you can force your way in as there are several ways and schemes that exist today, but being sustainable and comfortable will be quite difficult. If the mango tree were to force its way through the ground and sprout in December, it would have to face the harsh conditions of winter and limited sunlight, which would lead to its untimely and early demise.

BEWARE OF SHORTCUTS

Chance's quote about shortcuts always convicts me when I listen to it. We are so fixated on entering the game and arena of our lives that we will often do anything to get there. We will invest more, pay large amounts, and might even push someone else out of the way in order to arrive at what we deem as success. We definitely consider unethical avenues in order to attain what we feel belongs to us. However, all of these are feeble attempts to create a shortcut. No one likes to take the long way, especially when you just want to get home after a long day at work. Everyone desires to find the quickest, easiest, and most convenient way, yet what we fail to realize is that shortcuts can cut short long runs. There is a reason why the names Michael Jackson and Beyoncé are well known. Everyone knows their craft and their artistry is respected and admired. They didn't arrive on such pedestals by luck or chance, but by hard work, persistence, and taking the long road. The shortcut mindset says practice for 2 hours and call it a day 'cause you're already rich. The long-run mindset says practice all day until it's perfect and then wake up early in the morning and do it again before the show. The shortcut mindset encourages you to just skim the lines or let you just pull out the air fryer to cook while the long-run mindset says to memorize the lines until you can repeat them in your sleep.

Shortcuts do appear fun and are easy—that's why they are so popular—but shortcuts don't build greatness. Shortcuts don't create sustainable talent that goes on for decades. It's important to remember that shortcut opportunities will present themselves in various forms. While they may look harmless or simple, remember why you want to enter the game and for how long you want to be in the game. Do you want to be a one-hit wonder or do you want to be a household name? Do you want to be just another leader or a transformational leader that forever changes the course of the game? Arnold Glasow once said, "The key to everything is patience. You get the chicken by hatching the egg, not by smashing it." Patience plays a large role in achieving long-term success.

Kobe Bryant did not take shortcuts, even though he could have rested on his laurels. He won enough rings, collected enough accolades, yet every day until his last year playing, he gave the sport his all. As he avoided the shortcuts, he prolonged his career and will forever be memorialized. If you want to just be another person who entered the arena, then take all the shortcuts you want, but if you want to be a respected veteran and change how the game is played, avoid shortcuts at all costs.

How to Know When to Enter

I hope you see the many reasons why being patient and waiting for the right time is important in order to truly enter the game. It is one of the simple steps that we often overlook or ignore, but serves as the main catalyst to success. I would like to touch on a key part that I briefly mentioned: how to know when to enter. You're probably like, "I get it, I get it, I have to be patient and wait for the right window, but when will I know it's the right time!!?" Many people say things like "you just know" or "you go for it," but I believe we're actually called to the game. You are on the bench and you're watching, strategizing, practicing, and having the right attitude, but there's one person that makes a difference and is actually responsible for getting you into the game: The coach. There is a Coach in all of our lives that manages who enters the game and who sits on the bench. A Coach that provides pointers and chance after chance to every player whether or not they acknowledge His presence. It is the Coach who truly speaks to you and beckons you when your time has arrived. Similar to how my cousin yelled "Now!" we all have that voice in our head, that exterior voice of reasoning that seems to nudge us and move us toward feats we believed were impossible. In my personal opinion and belief, the Coach is God. He sets the seasons of the earth and also sets the seasons of our lives. The time set aside for watching, learning, strategizing, practicing, and even the time for entering and exiting the game. He is the One that really controls who gets off the bench, who gets to play, and for how long they play. A pastor once said, "We never know at what quarter we will be called to come out of the game. Some may play two quarters; others may play five minutes." We can all argue and complain about the unfairness in time, but truthfully, only the Coach knows and understands the game and the strengths that each player brings. He may bring in someone for a specific purpose and someone else for a lifetime of service. It's similar to heroes such as Dr. Martin Luther King Jr and John Lewis. Both were gifted and passionate black men who fought for justice, civil rights, and equality for all people. Yet one lived to be 39 (King) and the other 80 (Lewis). We can only speculate if the roles were reversed or if one was given more or less time, but it is feasible for us to see the evidence left behind by their fruits, legacy, and work toward progress. MLK had a specific purpose and calling, while John Lewis was called to a lifetime of consistent service. As a result, we don't know when that moment will come or for how long we will be in the game. It would be wise for us to look toward the Coach for our moment to enter the arena of our lives. Any attempt on our own will only lead to regret and misery.

"When you are on your beds, search your hearts and be silent" (Psalm 4:4 NIV). Take time to settle your mind and spirit and just listen. God is always speaking to us, but we often have the volume of the other areas of our lives so high we cannot or choose not to hear Him. The volume of comparison, the volume of critics and other people giving their opinions, and the volume of our dreams and fantasies can be so deafening that we don't hear the nudges or the restraint that the Coach is giving. Until we prioritize hearing His voice, we will always be lost and out of sync about when to enter the game. Don't enter until you receive that call.

REFLECTIONS FROM THIS CHAPTER

_____

_____

_____

_____

_____

_____

_____

_____

_____

_____

_____

_____

_____

The Defining Moment

"The Lord said to him, 'Who gives man his mouth? Who makes him deaf or dumb? Who gives him sight or makes him blind? It is I, the Lord. Now, go! I will help you to speak, and I will tell you what to say.'"

—Exodus 4:11–12 NIV

"In your life's defining moments there are two choices—you either step forward in faith and power or you step backward into fear."

—James Arthur Ray

"Grand-Jean!! You're in!" "You talking to me, Coach??" "Is there another Grand-Jean on this team?! Don't make me change my mind!" It was finally happening. Yet it was one of the scariest situations to enter. It was the last game

93

of the season, 4th quarter, with 6 minutes on the clock, our possession. We were trading points with the other team nearly the whole game and couldn't maintain a lead. Our star players were either tired or injured. Regardless of the reason, I was nervous and excited to get in the game and make a difference. It was now time for me to put into action everything I saw and studied in order to make it all count. It was as if time slowed down and everything went quiet. All I could hear was my heartbeat with every step I took. As I walked over to the scorer's table to sub in for my teammate, I began to address my mind-set and attitude, reaffirming my talent and abilities. "You're a great player, your team needs you, you've been made for this moment," I kept repeating to myself. I then began to recall what happened in the game and the weaknesses that our team had and the holes in the opposing team. I developed a strategy and realized how I could protect our team and add pressure on the other team. We were taking shots but would never get the rebound. I flashed back to the rebound techniques from practice and knew this was the time to implement them. The referee blew the whistle, handed me the ball, and the clock began to count down . . .

We all have a defining moment in our lives. The moment when the coach finally puts you in. The moment you meet the person who can take your business or talent to the next level. The moment where you're face-to-face with your destiny. You held a positive attitude and mindset, watched and took countless notes of the game, warmed up and practiced longer than usual, avoided shortcuts, and waited for the moment you were called. It's exciting, but pretty scary. It's finally what you asked for, but when you're face-to-face with the moment, it's intimidating. You get cold feet, your stomach is deciding to empty everything out, your mouth gets dry, and you feel dizzy. While these feelings are normal and common even to the most talented and prepared individuals, there is a key reason why we feel this way. We're afraid of blowing the opportunity.

No one wants to be the person who finally makes it to the dream stage only to embarrass themselves, their team, and their family. I'm sure you've seen countless videos on YouTube of athletes who make it to the Olympics only to mess up due to a false start, tripping on a hurdle, not being able to lift the weights, or finishing in last place. We're afraid that our positive attitude, countless hours watching the game, strategies, warm-ups, and waiting our turn will all be for nothing. As a result, we run away, or we make some excuse on why we can't step up to the challenge or moment. Instead of getting in the game once the coach calls our name, we make an excuse or we act like we didn't hear our name. There are many people that have missed their defining moment out of fear. Their fear of the task at hand is so great that they choose not to even make the attempt. This applies in more fields and areas than you know. There are men who are afraid of the defining moment of being a father so they leave or walk out of their marriage and commitment. There are women who have capabilities of owning and operating billion-dollar corporations but are afraid of being too intimidating to marry so they hide their ambitions and settle. There are men and women who have the talent and ability to cure diseases, lead nations, entertain millions, and provide invaluable products and services, but fear causes them to miss their defining moment. Fear tells them that it's impossible. Fear reminds them of their weaknesses and failures. Fear reminds them of the last time they tried to be great and how it was a waste of time. Fear stifles their confidence, diminishes their attitude, causes them to forget their notes and footage, lose their strategy, and discombobulate their warm-ups. Fear causes them to watch their defining moment slip by and the award goes to someone else.

One evening, my brothers and I decided to go to a concert in Atlanta for a guy date night. The tickets were cheap and we met two of my brother's friends so it was a recipe for a great night. We finally entered the venue and the artist began to perform. We were all excited, getting hyped, and vibing to the music. I casually looked behind me and just 3 feet away was a girl who locked eyes with me. Her eyes were captivating and seemed to sparkle casually as she smiled at me. I quickly turned my head back, focusing on the artist. "Maybe she was smiling at someone else— it couldn't be me," I said to myself. I happened to look back again, and once again she was looking at me, smiling, and was talking to her friend. "OK, OK, maybe she's just being friendly or thinks I'm weird for looking back," I said to myself. I decided to look back again after exactly 45 seconds to prove if it was just a coincidence. This time she smiled and waved at me and I promise I think she winked too. I blushed, waved, and turned around. I couldn't really focus on the concert anymore. "It's either now or never, bro. She definitely likes you and is LITERALLY inviting you to talk to her," my mind yelled at me. I started making excuses. "I don't know, maybe it's someone else. She's way out of my league. What if she laughs at me? I don't know if our personalities would match. Did I brush my teeth today?" I was having a world war in my mind over whether I should go and say hello or if I should stay put. I wanted to say something, but I was too afraid. In that moment, I was afraid of rejection, not getting her number, or just looking stupid. "OK, if you turn back again and she's looking at you, then you'll walk over to her," I finally agreed with my conscience. I looked back—and she was no longer there. I searched all over the venue, but couldn't find her. I began to pray frantically to God, begging that If I saw her again I wouldn't let my fear stop me.

Finally, I saw her, and my heart was relieved. She was smiling and laughing. As I began to make my way toward her, my heart turned cold and my feet stopped immediately. She was smiling and laughing with one of my brother's friends. I was too late. I had missed my defining moment because I was too afraid and allowed fear to immobilize me. When the concert was over, my brother's friend bragged about her amazing personality, getting her number, and even a good-night kiss. All I could do was smile and appear happy for him even though I was cursing myself in my head.

While that is a funny and amusing story of how fear often causes us to miss our defining moment, it can become more serious than not getting someone's number. We allow fear to rob us of ascending to that next level. We listen to our doubts more than our encouragement. Have you noticed that you remember insults more than you do compliments? For some reason, we wire our brain to remember the negatives and forget the positives of ourselves. We replay those childhood insults in our head over and over until we believe them and we miss out on our opportunity to achieve greatness.

You've probably heard the saying that success is a mindset. Most of what we do and achieve, if not *everything*, starts with our mind and mental aspect. The state of our mind determines if, and how well, we accomplish a task. When we allow negative thoughts, whether internal or external, to infiltrate our mind, they plant a seed that grows into weeds in our mind. At times, we also choose to water the negative thoughts over the positive thoughts until they grow into large weeds. These weeds at first seem harmless until they wrap themselves around the positive thoughts, which, if allowed to flourish, would give birth to flowers. Our negativity then suffocates our positivity, which affects our confidence and finally our performance. Be mindful of what you water, encourage, and endorse. Choose to be intentional with what you allow into your mind and the amount of time you dwell on each subject. The more you focus on the fear of the task in front of you, the more you begin to make it powerful and thus overwhelm the courage and bravery that lies within you. The cure is to remove the reason behind your fear.

One of the most memorable and inspiring quotes was delivered by President Theodore Roosevelt in a speech in France.

"It is not the critic who counts; not the man who points out how the strong man stumbles, or where the doer of deeds could have done them better. The credit belongs to the man who is actually in the arena, whose face is marred by dust and sweat and blood; who strives valiantly; who errs, who comes short again and again, because there is no effort without error and shortcoming; but who does actually strive to do the deeds; who knows great enthusiasms, the great devotions; who spends himself in a worthy cause; who at the best knows in the end the triumph of high achievement, and who at the worst, if he fails, at least fails while daring greatly, so that his place shall never be with those cold and timid souls who neither know victory nor defeat."

We need to remove our fear of losing and failing, and instead be honored and excited to be in the arena. You see, the credit, honor, and clout belongs to the person who actually joins the game. Who responds to the call. Who decides to serve their country in the midst of uncertainty. Who decides to step up and be a parent to an orphan. Who decides to open a business in the midst of a pandemic. Simply striving toward the goal and getting your hands involved in the arena you've been called to is what matters. It's bigger than accolades and records. It's bigger than your name being in lights, and it's bigger than even winning the game. It's about fulfilling the role you've been called to play and adding your mark and special abilities to the game. There will be shortcomings, pitfalls, frustrations, and even doubts, but those who strive valiantly are the ones who receive the prize. Once you decide to overcome fear and accept your call, you are already a winner. You're already a conqueror because you've decided that you will not allow your fear to cause you to miss your defining moment. Everything that happens afterwards is just details. Think about it. Whether you know or never heard of Jarrett Jack

doesn't change the fact that he's a professional basketball player and played in the NBA. We get so caught
up in being number one, featured on the cover of
TIME magazine, or being on the *Forbes* list of wealth-
iest individuals. While we should strive to be the best
version of ourselves, don't forget the true credit and
honor is simply getting the opportunity to be in your
element and do what you love. Deciding to put away
your fears and accept the call is what makes you great.

As Roosevelt closed perfectly with, you don't want
to be amongst "those cold and timid souls who neither know victory nor defeat." There are many people
who fit in that category. Who never accepted the call.
Who passed it to someone else because they thought
that they weren't ready or qualified. Or those who are
so afraid of defeat that they choose not to partici-
pate at all. Even the losers are arguably remembered
and admired for their tenacity and grit. Our love and
desire to get in the game has to be greater than our
desire to just win or our fear of losing. We have to
desire to be in the game to add value to the arena and
to put on a show for those to watch and cheer on. You
may feel as if your talent is not being noticed, that

every single law school rejects your application, or that you're the only one single in your friend group, but you cannot allow what you see now to deter you from entering the arena. You never know when you'll be called into the game, you never know which song will take off, you never know which application will be accepted, and you never know who will be your student or your patient. As a result, we need to take the defining moment seriously and put away the fear that easily entangles us and the doubts we hear and press on toward being our best in the arena.

NOW OR NEVER

The shot clock was counting down. I quickly passed the ball to my teammate and began to put my strategy in action. We weren't being aggressive enough in rebounds and so I made it my duty to go after every rebound and loose ball. As a result, we were able to regain possession and began to pull away. I noticed the star player on the opposing team kept scoring and tying the game. "I got him!" I yelled as I rushed toward him playing defense. He laughed once he saw me approaching him and began showing out. He darted left only to fake right as my legs got crossed and I fell to the floor. "Down goes Liston," he said as he stepped past me and made another bucket. The crowd went wild and even my own teammates snickered at each other. My knees were scuffed, but I got up and ran down the court to help with offense. We lost the possession, and once again I ran to play defense. "Coming back for more!?" he mocked as he began to shuffle. He jumped and drained a 3 in my face. The crowd went into an uproar and my teammates were hiding their faces in their jerseys. There was 2 minutes left on the clock and surprisingly the coach left me in the game. I wanted to feel discouraged and take myself out, but I remembered that it was my defining moment and that I wouldn't go out sad. Whether we won or lost, I wanted to leave it all on the court and prove to myself that I was more capable than I thought. We had possession and my teammate shot an open 3. The ball spun out, but I grabbed the rebound and put it back. The bench clapped as the coach gave a nod of approval. We were back on defense and I went back for thirds against the guy who was schooling me the whole night. He began to get cocky and woo the crowd with fancy dribbling. He went up for the layup, but I jumped up and blocked his shot into the stands. The bench went wild and "oooohs" could be heard from the crowd. My teammate passed me the ball and I sank a 3 with less than 1 minute left to go. The score was tied with 30 seconds on the clock. The whole crowd stood to their feet to watch and cheer as the game would finally be decided. We were back on defense. The opposing team tried to waste time with the ball and started passing as if they were the Harlem Globetrotters. It was hard for me to see who had the ball until the person I was defending shot an open 3. As the ball went down through the hoop, so did my confidence. I was doing well and was so close, but now it seemed as if the end was inevitable.

The score was 68-65 with 12 seconds to go. Coach called a time-out and pulled us together. "You guys are playing great. We're still in this game," he said. I began to tune out and was focusing on my mistake. I was in my own head beating myself up until I heard, "We're going to pass the ball to Grand-Jean and set him up for a three." I was confused, dumbfounded, and thought I was dreaming. "W-wait, who?? Come on, Coach, there's no way!" I protested. "We trust you, we've practiced for this moment, you can do it." I tried to continue my rant of excuses, but the time-out clock rang and everyone looked at me and gave me a nod. As I walked back on the court, I could sense the pressure of the whole school on me. I wasn't even that good, a third-string player, but here they were trusting me during the final seconds. I had to real-ize that while the last seconds would determine who would win the game, it was more than just winning for me. It was about getting the opportunity to play in front of my family, friends, and school and make a memorable moment. The whistle blew. My teammate inbounded the ball. The clock began to go down. I ran to get in position, and when my teammate tried to pass me the ball, it was intercepted by the opposing team. I shook my head, knowing the game was over, espe-cially with just 7 seconds left. Yet, in a split second, my teammate knocked the ball away from the oppos-ing player, and it came in my direction. I grabbed the ball and shot it, blinded by a defender jumping in front of me. I fell to the ground as the clock went off. My teammates began shouting and jumping off the bench. The crowd was restless. Apparently, I made the 3 and drew a foul in the process. The score was tied at 68. I took a breath and walked up to the foul line. The crowd was silent. I imagined myself back at practice and made the basket. 69-68. Game over. The crowd went wild and ran on the court. My teammates ran toward me and lifted me up on their shoulders. A cheerleader blew a kiss to me and told me to call her. It was the perfect ending to the last game of the season. Suddenly, I felt water hit my face. I thought it was Gatorade until I heard, "Ammishaddai!! Wake up! You're late for school!" I woke up in my pajamas seeing my mom with a bottle of water and a belt in her other hand.

REFLECTIONS FROM THIS CHAPTER

_____

_____

_____

_____

_____

_____

_____

_____

_____

_____

_____

_____

_____

Remember

"Have I not commanded you? Be strong and courageous. Do not be frightened, and do not be dismayed, for the lord your God is with you wherever you go."

—Joshua 1:9 ESV

"What matters in life is not what happens to you, but what you remember and how you remember it."

—Gabriel García Márquez

Congratulations!! You've reached the end of the book (or you skipped to the end to get a summary). You finally have all the tools and advice you need while you're on the bench waiting for your moment in the game. Eventually, we arrive in our desired arena of life and God has blessed us with the opportunity to live out our dreams, but before you go and enjoy your new income, celebrity status, or new spouse, know that the lights of the arena, the press conferences, and the endorsement deals can cause you to get lost in your new calling. Having a busier and more demanding schedule, added on with the expectation to always perform at 100 percent, is difficult. As a result, there is little time dedicated toward remembering the lessons and skills you picked up along the way. It's one thing to enter the game, but another thing to stay in the game for as long as you can. As a result, there are a couple things to remember.

REMEMBER YOUR ATTITUDE

Remember that a positive, humble, and hungry attitude got you to where you are and it will keep you where you are. Always continue to speak positivity over yourself and remind yourself of your value and uniqueness. Remember that a negative attitude can destroy your potential and gift as you aspire to join certain arenas of life. An arrogant and ungrateful attitude can also remove you from your dreams. Many people have been shut out and deserted due to their arrogance and lack of humility. Being cocky may seem to work in the beginning, but a humble spirit will take you further. Use your humility to uplift and mentor others. It's never fun being alone at the top. Finally, make sure that your attitude is not dependent on your performance. As time goes on, it is natural for your skills or special touch to change. That doesn't mean you're less valuable or talented. It means you have to be more creative on how you attain and achieve your goals. If your attitude is dependent on what you see, then you'll always feel unstable because one moment you're on top of the world and the next hour you feel at the bottom. Conversely, an attitude that is grounded in what you know is stable and consistent. Don't let your attitude escort you out of the game; instead, let your attitude elevate you.

REMEMBER TO WATCH THE GAME

Just because you're in the actual game doesn't mean that learning stops. There is always an opportunity to learn how to improve. You can always be a better spouse, parent, player, chef, actor, carpenter, or zoologist. Regardless of your profession, there is always a new development or a new skill that can improve your efficacy and prolong your tenure in the game. As LeBron progressed and became a veteran of the game, he didn't assume that he knew everything due to his experience and talent. He continued to watch the tapes of his game, but also the games of his younger opponents, and had to adjust and adapt in order to remain dominant. Despite how comfortable or secure you may feel in your new role in the arena, continue to read, learn, and even revisit your old notes in order to stay well versed and knowledgeable, thus adding to your skill set.

REMEMBER TO STRATEGIZE

It's important to always update and improve your strategy in order to remain efficient and perform at a high level. Your strategy may have got you into the arena and made you a major influencer, but eventually it has to change due to your new environment. Your strategy before was to just get in front of the camera and be a news reporter, but now your strategy has to shift toward how you can improve your skills in order to elevate and become a news anchor. Pay attention to the shifting trends of life. In the past, people relied on newspapers, but now social media is a major vehicle for information. You have to be creative and seek how to enter this new field and make it work to your advantage. This applies in all areas, including relationships. The strategy at first was to marry the person of your dreams. Once you attain that goal, your strategy has to shift toward how to keep the person of your dreams and how to improve yourself in order to maintain a healthy marriage. Your strategy will have to adapt once you're in your intended arena, so keep taking time to address it and make the necessary changes in order to continue to perform at the desired level.

REMEMBER TO PRACTICE

Continue to put thoughtful and intentional time toward practicing your craft. Remember the difference between Allen Iverson and Kobe Bryant. Do you want to be just another player, public servant, speaker, author, or do you want to become a household name that inspires others to do the same? Don't rest on your laurels and be content with getting into the game. Continue to spend time practicing and putting your strategy and lessons to work. This aids you in always being sharp and able to build upon your successes. Continue to practice that elevator pitch just in case you meet that next-level investor. Continue to try mixing new ingredients until you unlock that mind-blowing recipe. You'll be surprised and amazed at how much you can enhance your competence by remaining consistent in your routine.

REMEMBER NOT TO GO IN BEFORE YOU'RE CALLED

Life is all about timing. It's important to remember that life works in seasons and there is always an appointed time to make a move. There is a time for everything. Just because you have a new salary or a million-dollar contract doesn't mean you have to buy that BMW i8 or the largest house you can find. Always time your actions and decisions. Ensure the environment is stable and secure and that you've handled all unfinished business. There will be plenty of opportunities to elevate within your career, but remember to time it perfectly. There will also come a time when you want to exit and retire or change professions. Those decisions are fine, but remember not to leave too early. We often miss lessons and blessings because we move in haste and forget there are things to learn before we can levitate. Make sure to pray and be attuned to your desires and passions and aware of the environment you're in before you decide to make a strategic decision. Opportunities must align with your goals and values.

REMEMBER THE DEFINING MOMENT

You will mess up. *Yes, you actually will mess up.* You'll miss a meeting, miss a shot, or forget to add something. Contrary to popular belief, there is not one shot to make it. The defining moment is not bound by a single moment in time, but actually presents itself often. As a result, remember to always be prepared because you never know when that moment will happen. You never know when you'll run into the person who will change the course of your path. Always be prepared and continue to practice the skills and lessons you've accumulated. Remember to forgive yourself in case you do miss that moment or you mess up. It happens, but there will come another moment for you to show the world who you are. Finally, remember that life is bigger than just winning and losing. It is about the blessing of being able to hold the office, own a restaurant or business, and play in the game. The vast majority of people won't remember how many times you lost or botched an opportunity. Instead, they'll remember how you carried yourself, how you treated others, and how you entered and exited the arena. Your character is defined not by your mistakes, but your actions after your mistakes. It's about how you act when you're on top of the world and when you're at your wits' end. Enjoy and embrace the defining moment and the opportunity to be in the arena because there are those who are not as fortunate to know victory and defeat.

The final thing to remember is that you're not in control. Control is just an illusion. No one ever controls anything. Everything is given, ordained, and allowed by God, the Coach of life. He decides who gets to play, where they play, and for how long they play. He's the person that we must always strive to check in with and receive our marching orders and playbook from. Many choose to ignore Him and go through life on their own, but I believe they don't live to their full purpose in every part of their life beyond being under the lights of the arena. It's important to remember our Coach and trust that He sees and knows more than we could ever see or know, and that if we hold His hand, take time to listen, and follow His plan, we'll achieve and attain a glory that no person can take away or diminish. Being on the bench is hard, frustrating, and even draining, but similar to a mother who toils for 9 months and gives birth, you won't remember the struggle as much when you experience the moment you leave the bench.

Thank you so much for reading to the end. I pray that this book blesses, inspires, encourages, and guides you through your journey of being on the bench. I pray you will find comfort in this poem that fixes my gaze when I feel too low and humbles me when I get too high.

Remember your Creator
in the days of your youth,
before the days of trouble come
and the years approach when you will say,

"I find no pleasure in them"—
before the sun and the light
and the moon and the stars grow dark,
and the clouds return after the rain;
when the keepers of the house tremble,
and the strong men stoop,
when the grinders cease because they are few,
and those looking through the windows grow dim;
when the doors to the street are closed
and the sound of grinding fades;
when people rise up at the sound of birds,
but all their songs grow faint;
when people are afraid of heights
and of dangers in the streets;
when the almond tree blossoms
and the grasshopper drags itself along
and desire no longer is stirred.
Then people go to their eternal home
and mourners go about the streets.
Remember him—before the silver cord is severed,
and the golden bowl is broken;
before the pitcher is shattered at the spring,
and the wheel broken at the well,

and the dust returns to the ground it came from,
and the spirit returns to God who gave it.

—Ecclesiastes 12:1–7 NIV

REFLECTIONS FROM THIS CHAPTER

_____

_____

_____

_____

_____

_____

_____

_____

_____

_____

_____

_____

Acknowledgments

I'd like to thank God for gifting me the concept for the book and granting me the energy and wisdom to write this book. I literally remember the title falling in my head and feeling God impressing me to write it down and hold on to it. I never would've imagined that it would lead to an actual published book. I also would like to thank God for so many instances of saving me from myself and from so many situations. I pray that I made You proud and I look forward to seeing You face-to-face.

To my parents—Mom and Dad. My dad has written two books and I never thought I would join him as an author. Thank you for your life examples of resiliency and determination, and your animated bedtime stories when I was afraid of storms. Thanks for igniting a fire in me to serve God and accomplish His will for my life. To my beautiful, loving, and generous mother. I am in awe of the extent of love you show for our family. Your sacrifice knows no bounds. You are a selfless, caring, strong, and an intelligent black woman. I'll always cherish your proverbs and wise sayings.

To my siblings: Nashbi, Jonathan, and Sofia. Nashbi, mi hermano, my right hand, and confidant. Since birth you possessed a spirit and light that is pure and attracts those around you. I can't wait to see you win your first Grammy and get the recognition you deserve (listen to him on all platforms). Jonathan, you embody the Hebrew prince in whose name you bear. You are kind, sincere, filled with swag, and an influencer amongst your peers. You always build my confidence and support me in all my crazy endeavors. I know you'll achieve your dreams and make them a colorful reality. Sofia, the first princess and unexpected miracle child. You are intentional, comfortable in your own skin, talented beyond measure, and a natural leader. Thanks for believing in me and your pointers with girls. You will be a role model for your generation and I look forward to supporting you every step of the way.

My brother from another mother, Arthur. Never would I have imagined a car conversation would bloom to a strong relationship filled with laughter, wisdom, and a chess/spades rivalry. Thank you for your sacrifice, lessons, and friendship. It is apparent that God's hand is upon you and that you will be a leader that will turn the hearts of people back to Christ. My spiritual grandfather, mentor, and friend Chaplain Barry Black. You've taught me more in action than in words. Thank you for your wisdom, encouragement, hours of free counseling sessions, and providing me a home away from home. Your words and generosity toward me will forever remain etched in my mind. My spiritual grandfather, counselor, teacher, and friend Dr. Roland Hill. Thank you for speaking life into me since the day we met and being a constant supporter of all my endeavors. Your wisdom and prayers helped me through many toils and for that I'm eternally grateful.

To my special test subjects and friends: Destin, Aminah, Keturah, Sam, and Annisha. Thank you for reading the book for free, giving me your honest feedback without hurting my feelings, and for your moral support when I wanted to throw the computer away. I am blessed to call each of you friend.

To my beloved Haitian community. Thank you for your prayers, affirmation, tasty food, and vibrant spirit. You all inspire me and hold me accountable to be authentic to who God made me to be and to always carry my head high because we are royalty.

To the long list of institutions and organizations that include the many people who have helped me get to where I am. First Jonesboro Baptist Church, La Petite Academy, McGarrah Elementary, Brown Elementary, Mundy's Mill Middle, Elite Scholars Academy, Bethel Community SDA Church, Jerusalem Des Ondes, Adventist Christian Fellowship, BUGA, and the University of Georgia.

Finally to you, the reader. Thanks for picking up this book and reading it until the end. I pray that God will magnify the blessings in this book and add them to your life. I pray however long God decides to keep you on the bench that your faith will not fail, that your countenance will not fall, and that you become a source of encouragement to others. I pray that your time off the bench will be so sweet and fruitful that you will barely remember the pain and sorrows you went through. God bless you and please leave a review on Amazon, other online retailers, and connect with me on social media, @asgrandjean or agjspeaks.com, and let me know your candid thoughts. I'll see you in the game!

About the Author

Born to Haitian parents in the beautiful city of Jonesboro, Georgia, Ammishaddai Sully Grand-Jean was given a biblical name meaning "The Powerful God is my parent." Living up to the name, Ammishaddai seeks to make God proud and invigorate the minds of his generation. He has spoken in front of thousands of individuals, churches, schools, community events, and was invited by the CEO of Chick-fil-A, Dan Cathy, to deliver the Morning Devotion at their headquarters in Atlanta, Georgia. Ammishaddai delivers speeches in 3 languages: English, French, and Creole.

Ammishaddai specializes in Personal & Organizational Leadership, Growth & Development, Youth

Connection, and Strategic Communication. Ammishaddai finds great joy in connecting with his audience and awakening their determination of applying the lessons shared. Ammishaddai currently holds a master's in Public Administration, two bachelor's degrees in Economics and Political Science, and two certificates in Personal & Organizational Leadership and Local Government Administration from the University of Georgia. In his free time, he enjoys watching movies, shows, playing chess, spades, *Call of Duty*, and basketball. Ammishaddai enjoys interacting with fans and can be found on Instagram and Twitter at @ asgrandjean and www.agjspeaks.com.

Made in the USA
Middletown, DE
12 March 2021

35393796R00077